Russia
For Kids
People, Places and Cultures
Children Explore The World Books

SPEEDY
PUBLISHING

Speedy Publishing LLC
40 E. Main St. #1156
Newark, DE 19711
www.speedypublishing.com

Copyright 2015

Let's learn some interesting facts about Russia!

The official
name for Russia
is the Russian
Federation.

Russia shares borders with many countries—China, Ukraine, North Korea and Norway.

ussia

Russia was estimated to have a population of around 143 million.

Russia is the largest country in the world in terms of land area.

RUSSIA
Blagoveshchensk
Chita
Irkutsk

Amsterdam
NETH.
NORWAY
Oslo
SWEDEN
DENMARK
Copenhagen
GERMANY
Berlin
Stockholm
FINLAND
Helsinki
Barents Sea
NOVAYA ZEMLYA
Kara Sea
Murmansk
Prague
CZ. REP.
Baltic Sea
Tallinn
Kaliningrad
Riga
EST.
St.Petersburg
Karelia
SLOV.
POLAND
Warsaw
LITH.
LAT.
Vilnius
Pskov
Arkhangel'sk
Nenetsia
HUNG.
Minsk
Novgorod
BELARUS
Tver
Vologda
Komi
Permyakia
Yamalia
ROMANIA
Bucharest
MOLDOVA
Chisinau
UKRAINE
Smolensk
Kiev
Kaluga
Bryansk
Orel
Tula
Kutsk
Lipetsk
Ryazan
Belgorod
Voronezh
Yaroslavl
Kostroma
Ivanovo
Vladimir
Nizhniy Novgorod
Tambov
Penza
Kirov
Perm
Khantia-Mansia
Sverdlovsk
Yekaterinburg
Chelyabinsk
Tyumen
Bashkortostan
Ul'yanovsk
Samara
Tatarstan
Black Sea
Ankara
Rostov
Volgograd
Saratov
Orenburg
Kurgan
Omsk
Tomsk
Novosibirsk
TURKEY
GEORGIA
Tibilisi
Astrakhan
ARMENIA
Yerevan
SYRIA
AZERBAIJAN
Baku
Caspian Sea
KAZAKHSTAN
Altay
Aral Sea
Lake Balkhash
Gor Alta
IRAQ
UZBEKISTAN

Russia has 9 time zones across the country.

The capital
and largest
city in Russia
is Moscow.

The currency used in Russia is the ruble.

Russia is rich of natural resources and is one of the world's largest producers of oil.

The Soviet Union (USSR) was a socialist state that occupied much of northern Asia and eastern Europe from 1922 until it was dissolved in 1991.

The official residence of the Russian president is the Kremlin in Moscow which means fortress.

Russia has over 40 national parks and 100 wildlife reserves.

Lake Baikal is the largest freshwater lake in the world. It reaches 1642 metres (5,387 feet) in depth and contains around 20% of the world's unfrozen fresh water.

Mount Elbrus is the highest mountain in Russia (and Europe), it reaches a height of 5642 metres (18,510 feet).

Volga River is the longest in Europe, with a length of around 3690 kilometres (2293 miles).

Russia has the
world's largest
area of forests.

Russia produces a large amount of renewable energy.

Basketball, ice hockey and football are popular sports in Russia.

Russia has a lot to offer and you should visit the country soon and explore!

Visit

BABY PROFESSOR
EDUCATION KIDS

www.BabyProfessorBooks.com
to download Free Baby Professor eBooks
and view our catalog of new and exciting
Children's Books

www.ingramcontent.com/pod-product-compliance
Lightning Source LLC
Chambersburg PA
CBHW060145120726

48003CB00009B/3023